SOUTH AFRICA

A VISUAL SOUVENIR

Struik Publishers (Pty) Ltd
(a member of Struik New Holland Publishing (Pty) Ltd)
80 McKenzie Street, Cape Town 8001
Reg. No.: 54/00965/07

ISBN 1 86872 053 5

First published in 1999
Copyright © in published edition:
Struik Publishers (Pty) Ltd 1999
Copyright © in photographs: 1999 as credited opposite

Managing editor: Annlerie van Rooyen
Design manager: Janice Evans
Designer: Sonia Hedenskog de Villiers
Text: Glynne Newlands
French translator: Cécile Spottiswoode
German translator: Friedel Herrmann

Reproduction: Disc Express Cape (Pty) Ltd
Printing: Tien Wah Press (Pte) Limited, Singapore

2 4 6 8 10 9 7 5 3 1

A fisherman's cottage at St Helena Bay on the West Coast (front cover). Ricksha driver in Durban (spine). Kruger cheetah (back cover). Bathing huts at St James beach, Cape Town (title page). The Knysna Heads and Lagoon, Garden Route (right).

Une maison de pêcheur à St Helena Bay sur la Côte Ouest (couverture recto). Conducteur de pousse-pousse à Durban (dos). Guépard au Kruger (couverture verso). Cabines de bain à St James (page de titre). La lagune de Knysna sur la Route des Jardins (à droite).

Eine Fischerkate in St. Helena Bay an der Westküste (Umschlagbild) Rickschafahrer in Durban (Kante) Gepard in der Kruger (Buchrücken) Badehäuschen am Strand von St. James, Kapstadt (Titelseite) Knysna-Lagune, Gartenroute (rechts).

INTRODUCTION

South Africa's remarkable diversity is clearly visible in its nine provinces, each possessing a character and beauty of its own, be it in its people, its landscapes, its wildlife or its culture.

INTRODUCTION

L'extraordinaire diversité de l'Afrique du Sud apparaît très clairement dans ses neuf provinces. Chacune d'entre elles possède un caractère et une beauté uniques que reflètent ses habitants, ses paysages, sa vie sauvage ou sa culture.

EINLEITUNG

Südafrikas bemerkenswerte Vielfalt tritt deutlich zutage in seinen neun Provinzen, jede mit charakteristischen Merkmalen und eigener Schönheit, ausgebildet in den Menschen, dem Wildleben und den Landschaften oder in der Kultur.

Zulu homes at the foothills of the imposing Drakensberg range (left) in KwaZulu-Natal.

Habitations zouloues au pied du Drakensberg (à gauche) au KwaZulu-Natal.

Heimstätten der Zulu am Fuße der Drakens-berge in KwaZulu-Natal (links).

*The summit of Table Mountain (right), Cape Town's most famous landmark, is easily
accessed by foot or by cable car (above).*

*Le sommet de la Montagne de la Table (à droite), site le plus célèbre du Cap, est facilement accessible
à pied ou en téléphérique (ci-dessus).*

*Auf den Tafelberg (rechts), dem berühmten Wahrzeichen Kapstadts, kann man ohne Schwierigkeiten
kommen, entweder zu Fuß oder mit derSeilbahn (oben).*

Cape Town's lively markets, such as the Grand Parade (opposite), the Adderley Street flower sellers (above) and Cape Minstrels (top right) bring sound and colour to this cosmopolitan city.

Les marchés du Cap: au "Grand Parade" (ci-contre) et à Adderley Street avec ses marchandes de fleurs (ci-dessus). Les musiciens du Carnaval du Cap (en haut à droite) apportent gaieté et pittoresque à la ville.

Kapstadts geschäftige Märkte – wie auf der Grand Parade (gegenüber) – und die Blumenverkäufer der Adderley Street (oben) oder die Cape Minstrels (oben rechts) bringen Klang und Farbe in das Stadtbild.

The Victoria & Alfred Waterfront (left), one of the Cape's premier tourist
venues, is the departure point for ferry trips (above) to Robben Island.

Le Victoria & Alfred Waterfront (à gauche), l'un des premiers sites touristiques du Cap,
est le point de départ pour prendre le ferry (ci-dessus) pour Robben Island.

Die Victoria & Alfred Waterfront (links), eine der größten Touristenattraktionen am Kap, ist die
Abfahrtsstelle für die Fährschiffe (oben) nach Robben Eiland.

Cape Town is blessed with many beautiful beaches. Here, Lion's Head forms a dramatic backdrop to Camps Bay beach (right).

Le Cap est dotée de magnifiques plages. Ici, Lion's Head domine majestueusement la plage de Camps Bay (à droite).

Kapstadt ist mit vielen herrlichen Stränden gesegnet. Hier bildet der Löwenkopf eine Kulisse für den Strand bei Camps Bay (rechts).

Fishermen unload their catch at Hout Bay harbour (left). From here a drive along Chapman's Peak (opposite) affords spectacular views of the Atlantic seaboard.

Des pêcheurs déchargent leurs chalutiers au port de Hout Bay (à gauche). A partir d'ici, la route panoramique de Chapman's Peak (ci-contre) offre des vues saisissantes sur l'Atlantique.

Im Hafen von Hout Bay bringen Fischer ihre Fracht ein (links). Eine Küstenstraße führt am Chapman's Peak entlang (gegenüber) mit atemberaubenden Aussichten auf die Atlantikküste.

The Cape of Good Hope Nature Reserve, which encompasses Cape Point (opposite), is also known for its magnificent scenery, its flora and fauna, its excellent restaurant (above), and its lighthouse (top right).

La réserve naturelle du cap de Bonne Espérance qui inclut la Pointe du Cap (ci-contre), est aussi réputée pour ses magnifiques paysages, sa faune et sa flore, ses restaurants (ci-dessus) ainsi que pour son phare (en haut à droite).

Das Naturschutzgebiet Cape of Good Hope, das die Kapspitze (umseitig) einschließt, ist auch bekannt für seine wunderschöne Landschaft, Flora und Fauna, das ausgezeichnete Restaurant (oben) und den Leuchtturm (oben rechts).

Groot Constantia wine estate (above), built in the 17th century, and Kirstenbosch National Botanical Garden (right) provide peaceful escapes from the city's bustle.

Le domaine vinicole de Groot Constantia (ci-dessus), fondé au 17ème siècle. Le Jardin botanique national de Kirstenbosch (à droite), havre de paix à l'écart des foules.

Groot Constantia (oben), das Weingut aus dem 17. Jahrhundert, und Kirstenbosch National Botanischer Garten (rechts) bieten geruhsame Zufluchtsstätten von dem Trubel der Stadt.

Images of the Cape winelands: Oom Samie se Winkel in Stellenbosch (above), the French Huguenot Memorial, Franschhoek (top right) and the glorious Hex River Valley (opposite).

Images de la région vinicole: Oom Samie se Winkel à Stellenbosch (ci-dessus), le Mémorial aux Huguenots (en haut à droite) et la somptueuse vallée de la Hex (ci-contre).

Eindrücke aus dem Weinland am Kap: Oom Samie se Winkel in Stellenbosch (oben), das Hugenottendenkmal in Franschhoek (oben rechts) und das malerische Hex River Tal (umseitig).

Each spring, southern right whales come to calve in Hermanus's sheltered bays (left).
The lighthouse at Cape Agulhas marks the southernmost tip of Africa (above).

Chaque année au printemps, les baleines franches viennent mettre bas dans les baies abritées d'Hermanus
(à gauche). Le phare du cap Agulhas, situé à l'extrémité sud du continent africain (ci-dessus).

Im Frühjahr kommen Südliche Glattwale zum Kalben in die geschützten Buchten von Hermanus (links).
Der Leuchtturm von Kap Agulhas steht an der südlichsten Spitze von Afrika (oben).

The Outeniqua Choe-Tjoe (page 24) crosses the Kaaimans River en route to Wilderness (page 25) before continuing further up the Garden Route.

Le "Outeniqua Choe-Tjoe" (page 24) enjambe la Kaaimans et se dirige vers Wilderness (page 25) avant de continuer son trajet le long de la Route des Jardins.

Der Outeniqua Tschu-Tschu (Seite 24) dampft über den Kaaimans River in Richtung Wilderness (Seite 25) und dann weiter entlang der Gartenroute.

The popular resorts of Knysna (opposite) and
Plettenberg Bay (left) along the Garden Route.

*Les stations balnéaires à la mode: Knysna
(ci-contre) et Plettenberg Bay (à gauche) le long
de la Route des Jardins.*

*Die beliebten Feriendomizile Knysna (umseitig)
und Plettenberg Bay (links) liegen auf der
Gartenroute.*

After good rains, the arid Little Karoo (right)
is transformed into a lush, colourful landscape.

*Après des pluies abondantes, l'aride Petit Karoo
(à droite) se pare de multiples couleurs et se
transforme en un paysage luxuriant.*

*Nach guten Regen verwandelt sich die Kleine
Karru (rechts) in eine blühende Landschaft.*

In the Karoo, Oudtshoorn and its surrounds are ideally suited to ostrich and crocodile farming (above and top right). The spectacular Cango Caves (opposite) are also situated there.

Dans le Karoo, Oudtshoorn et ses terres environnantes sont réputées pour les élevages d'autruches et de crocodiles (ci-dessus et en haut à droite). Les extraordinaires grottes de Cango (ci-contre) se trouvent également ici.

Die Umgebung von Oudtshoorn in der Karru ist bestens geeignet für Straußen- und Krokodil-zucht (oben und rechts oben). Hier sind auch die beeindruckenden Cangohöhlen (umseitig), Kalksteinlabyrinthe riesigen Ausmaßes.

The Valley of Desolation in Graaff Reinet (left) and the Addo Elephant Park (above)
are two highlights of a visit to the Eastern Cape.

La vallée de la Désolation à Graaf-Reinet (à gauche) et le parc d'éléphants d'Addo (ci-dessus):
deux sites inoubliables lors d'une visite dans le Cap de l'Est.

Das Tal der Trostlosigkeit in Graaf Reinet (links) und der Addo Elefantenpark (oben) sind zwei
Höhepunkte bei einem Besuch im Ostkap

Port Elizabeth's leisure activities include sunbathing and watersports (opposite) and a visit to the Dolphinarium (top right). Its library (above), graced by Queen Victoria, is a well-known landmark.

A Port Elizabeth les sports nautiques (ci-contre) font le bonheur des estivants ainsi qu'une visite au parc océanographique, réputé pour ses dauphins (en haut à droite). Sa bibliothèque (ci-dessus), avec la statue de la reine Victoria.

Port Elisabeth bietet Freizeitgestaltung wie Sonnenbaden und Wassersport (umseitig) und einen Besuch im Delphinarium (oben rechts). Die Bibliothek (oben) mit der Königin Viktoria im Vordergrund ist ein bekanntes Wahrzeichen.

The Eastern Cape, the traditional home of the Xhosa (above), is also famed for its rolling
grassland and mountainous areas, such as the Katberg (right).

*Le Cap de l'Est, territoire traditionnel des Xhosas (ci dessus), est aussi célèbre pour ses collines
herbeuses et son relief montagneux, comme au Katberg (à droite).*

*Das Ostkap, die angestammte Heimat der Xhosa (oben), ist auch bekannt für seine Hügellandschaft
und Gebirge, wie der Katberg (rechts).*

*The sculpted beauty of Hole in
the Wall (right) along the Wild Coast.*

*La merveille naturelle du Hole in the Wall
(à droite) le long de la Côte Sauvage.*

*Das Felsmassiv Hole-in-the-Wall (rechts)
an der Wilden Küste.*

The vibrant faces of Durban: its yacht basin
(opposite), a ricksha driver (above) and an
Indian spice market (top right).

Les facettes de Durban: son port de plaisance
(ci-contre), un conducteur de pousse-pousse (ci-
dessus) et son marché aux épices (en haut à droite).

Durbans vielfältige Stadtszenen: der Jachthafen
(umseitig), ein Rickschafahrer (oben) und ein
indischer Gewürzmarkt (oben rechts).

Pietermaritzburg's grand City Hall (opposite).
The graceful tumble of Howick Falls (right) in
the KwaZulu-Natal Midlands.
The breathtaking Amphitheatre (pages 44 45)
forms part of the Drakensberg mountain range.

L'Hôtel de Ville majestueux de Pietermaritzburg
(ci contre). Les gracieuses chutes de Howick
(à droite) qui se trouvent dans les Midlands
au Kwazulu-Natal.
L'Amphithéâtre, panorama à vous couper le
souffle (pages 44-45), fait partie de la chaîne
du Drakensberg.

Der imposante Ratsaal von Pietermaritzburg
(umseitig). Graziös plätschern die Howickfälle
(rechts) in den Midlands von KwaZulu-Natal.
Das grandiose Amphitheater (Seite 44-45)
bildet Teil der Drakensberge.

Loteni camp (above) is idyllically situated in the Drakensberg. Zulu maidens at Shakaland in KwaZulu-Natal (opposite).

Le camp de Loteni (ci-dessus) au Drakensberg est situé dans un cadre idéal. Des jeunes filles zouloues à Shakaland au Kwazulu-Natal (ci-contre).

Loteni Camp (oben) ist idyllisch gelegen in den Drakensbergen. Zulumädchen in Shakaland in KwaZulu-Natal (umseitig).

Lake St Lucia (left) and Sodwana Bay – the breeding ground of endangered loggerhead turtles (above) –
form part of the beautiful Greater St Lucia Wetland Park.
Mpumalangu's spectacular Blyde River Canyon (pages 50–51).

Le lac de St Lucia (à gauche) et Sodwana Bay – lieu de reproduction des tortues luth (ci-dessus), espèce
en voie de disparition – fait partie du "Greater St Lucia Wetland Park", étonnante zone de marais.
Le canyon spectaculaire de la Blyde (pages 50-51) au Mpumalanga.

Der See St. Lucia (links) und die Sodwananbucht - Anlaufstelle der bedrohten Karettschildkröte (oben)-
bilden Teil des wunderbaren Greater St. Lucia Wetland Park.
Mpumalangas atemberaubender Blyde River Canyon (Seite50/51)

The historic mining town of Pilgrim's Rest
(above) and the lovely Berlin Falls (opposite)
in Mpumalanga.

Pilgrim's Rest, ancien village minier (ci-dessus)
ainsi que les belles chutes de Berlin (ci-contre)
au Mpumalanga.

Das historische Minendorf Pilgrim's Rest (oben)
und die bezaubernden Berlinfälle (umseitig)
in Mpumalanga.

Scenes of the Kruger National Park: lion
(opposite), one of the Big Five, and giraffe at
a waterhole (above).

Scènes prises au parc national Kruger: un lion
(ci-contre), l'un des Cinq Grands, et des girafes
qui s'abreuvent (ci-dessus).

Szenen im Krugerpark: ein Löwe (umseitig),
er gehört zu den Großen Fünf, und Giraffen
an der Wasserstelle (oben).

Olifants rest camp (right) provides the perfect base from which to explore central Kruger Park.

Le camp d'Olifants (à droite) constitue une base idéale pour explorer la partie centrale du parc Kruger.

Das Olifants Rastlager (rechts) ist ein ausgezeichneter Ausgangspunkt um den mittleren Teil des Krugerparks zu erkunden.

Nighttime softens Johannesburg's skyline (left).
The city is a cosmopolitan, exciting metropolis.

La ligne d'horizon de Johannesburg (à gauche),
adoucie par la nuit. La ville est une métropole
dynamique et cosmopolite.

Bei Nacht verlieren die Umrisse der Skyline
von Johannesburg (links) ihre harten und
abweisenden Züge. Die Stadt ist eine kosmopoli-
tische, pulsierende Metropole.

The Hartebeespoort Dam (opposite) and mine dancing at Gold Reef City (right) are two of Gauteng's main attractions.
The Union Buildings (pages 62–63) are superbly positioned overlooking South Africa's capital city, Pretoria.

Le barrage de Hartebeespoort (ci-contre) et le spectacle de danses sur les mines à Gold Reef City (à droite) caractérisent la région du Gauteng.
Les Union Buildings (pages 62-63), édifices magnifiquement situés, surplombent Pretoria, capitale du pays.

Der Hartebeespoort-Stausee (umseitig) und die Minentänze in Gold Reef City (rechts) gehören zu den Attraktionen von Gauteng.
Die Union Buildings (Seite 62/63) sind hervorragend plaziert mit Blick auf die Hauptstadt Südafrikas, Pretoria.

Pretoria is aptly known as the Jacaranda
City (opposite).
The Ndebele are renowned for their geometric
designs and colourful murals and attire
(above and top right).

Pretoria qui mérite bien son nom de "Ville des
Jacarandas" (ci-contre). Les Ndebeles sont
réputes pour leurs motifs géométriques, leurs
peintures murales aux vives couleurs et leur
habit traditionnel (ci-dessus et en haut à droite).

Pretoria ist zu recht bekannt als die
Jakarandastadt (gegenüber).
Die Ndebele sind berühmt für ihre geometrischen
Motive in der farbenfrohen Wandmalerei und der
traditionellen Kleidung (oben und obe rechts).

The Valley of the Waves at Sun City (left) and the lavish Palace of the Lost City (opposite) are both located in the North-West Province.

La "Vallée des Vagues" à Sun City (à gauche) et l'opulent "Palace" de Lost City (ci-contre) se trouvent tous deux dans la province du Nord-Ouest.

Das Tal der Wellen in Sun City (links) und der luxuriöse Palast von Lost City (umseitig) liegen beide in der Nordwestprovinz.

*Fields of golden sunflowers (pages 68–69)
garnish the Free State's plains.
A typical scene of Clarens (left), a picturesque
town in the Free State.*

*Des champs de soleils aux teintes dorées
(pages 68-69) parent les plaines de l'Etat libre.
Vue caractéristique de Clarens (á gauche), ville
pittoresque de l'Etat libre.*

*Goldene Sonnenblumenfelder (Seite 68/69)
überziehen die Ebenen im Freistaat.
Typische Landschaft bei Clarens (links), einem
malerischen Ort im Freistaat.*

A Basotho village (left), with typically colourful designs, near Clarens in the Free State.
Kimberley's Big Hole (above). When it closed in 1914, some three tons of diamonds had been mined.

Village basotho (à gauche), et ses de motifs typiques, près de Clarens dans l'Etat libre.
Kimberley et son "Grand Trou" (ci-dessus). A sa fermeture en 1914, on en avait extrait trois tonnes de diamants.

Ein Basothodorf (links) mit den typischen, farbigenfreudigen Motiven in der Nähe von Clarens im Freistaat.
Das Große Loch bei Kimberley (oben). Bis 1914 wurden dort etwa dreitausend Tonnen Diamanten gefördert.

The Kalahari Gemsbok National Park was
created to protect the graceful gemsbok (left).
The Orange River bordering the Richtersveld
(page 76) flows through the Northern Cape
before narrowing to form the thunderous
Augrabies Falls (page 77).

Le parc national du Kalahari Gemsbok a
été créé pour protéger l'élégante antilope oryx
(à gauche).
Le fleuve Orange qui borde la région du
Richtersveld (page 76) traverse la province
Nord du Cap puis il se rétrécit et forme les
tumultueuses chutes d'Augrabies (page 77).

Der Kalahari Gembok Nationalpark wurde ins
Leben gerufen, um die graziöse Oryxantilope
zu schützen (links).
Der Oranjefluß grenzt an das Richtersveld
(Seite 76) und fließt durch das Nordkap, ehe
er schmaler wird und die donnernden
Augrabiesfälle bildet (Seite 77).

A riot of spring flowers at Goegap Nature
Reserve (page 78) near Springbok.
The Wolfberg Arch in the Cedarberg (page 79).

Un tapis éclatant de fleurs printanières dans
la réserve naturelle de Goegap (page 78) près
de Springbok.
L'arche de Wolfberg dans la région du
Cedarberg (page 79).

Im Goegap Naturschutzgebiet bei Springbok
(Seite 78) schmücken eine Vielzahl bunter
Frühlingsblumen das Feld.
Bogenfels am Wolfberg in den Zederbergen
(Seite 79).

Fishing boats at the village of Paternoster along the West Coast (page 80).

Cape gannets at Lambert's Bay (endpapers).

Des bateaux de pêche à Paternoster le long de la Côte Ouest (page 80).

Des fous du Cap à Lambert's Bay (pages de titre).

Fischerboote bei Paternoster an derWestküste (Seite 80).

Kaptölpel bei Lamberts Bay (Vorsatzblatt).